Beautiful Bread

To Owen
a "Great Man"

from Christopher
R. Endler.

Beautiful Bread
Baking with Spelt

Natures Healthy Alternative

Nature's wholegrain goodness tastes amazing . . .
Nourishing and Nutritious.

By
The Wandering Chef
Christopher Robin Endler

To order additional copies of this book, contact:
Xlibris Corporation
1-888-795-4274
www.Xlibris.com
Orders@Xlibris.com
34441

Contents

Foreword

My background in the culinary world represents over 25 years of experience at a variety of restaurants, most of them specializing in creative gourmet fine dining. I have also cooked for celebrities, and performed numerous outside catering functions and special events.

My nutritional studies have lead me to a greater understanding of the great need for people to make available for themselves nourishing, great tasting breads in a world where devitalized foods have become so common place. It is my intention to empower others to help themselves in the art of fine baking, blending old world flavors with the freshest ingredients available today.

Acknowledgements

A special note of thanks to research contact for references and information is extended to the following:

Vita Spelt—Purity Foods, Leonard Ridzon of Ridzon Farms, Hildegard of Bingham, and Dr. Wighard Stehlon. Also very special thanks to Georgos Hatonn and the Contact newspaper in providing invaluable information on the history and use of spelt and its wonders.

Products, Information, and Sources of Spelt available:

Purity Foods, Inc
2871 W. Jolly Road
Okemos, MI 48804
(517) 351-9231

Ridzon Farms
47810 Star Route 14
New Waterford, OH 44445
(800) 289-3636

Spelt (*triticum spelta*)

♦ Important Grain
♦ Mysterious Healing Qualities
♦ As Dietary Supplement
♦ One of the most Nutritious Grains, a Whole Food Source

Triticum spelta is not wheat. It is one of the most original and natural grains known to modern research, which has proven that spelt has been grown widely for more than 9,000 years. Spelt was also documented in early medieval Europe in the 10th century by Hildegcird of Bingham, an early nun of famous reputation for her herbal and health giving remedies using spelt in the daily intake of food stuffs.

Spelt contains all of the basic materials for a healthy diet including protein, fats, carbohydrates, vitamins, supplements, and minerals. Spelt also has special carbohydrates (muco-polysoccharides) which play a central role in blood-clotting and stimulating the body's immune system as well as essential amino acids that our bodies cannot produce. Spelt is a hard grain type of wheat but not wheat per se. In fact, those with wheat allergies are not affected by spelt varieties. There are four main kinds of spelt, however the spelt referred to as common spelt is the most nutritious and the only one which carries large amounts of vitamin B-7 (anticancer). It is the grain God gave to the plant as "manna" when you were put on it.

I am making no health claims other than as a dietary supplement of a healthy grain, a great fiber resource. Spelt has been called the staff of life in Europe for centuries. The French know it as epeautre, the Germans call it dinkel, and the

Italians revere it as faro. The spelta is more mildly flavorable than wheat, and even one who is allergic to wheat may have no allergy to spelt.

Along with the subject of grains for eating, naturally the subject of bread follows.

The baking of bread goes back to the dawn of civilization. Archaeological evidence of remains indicate that stone age residents of Europe were mixing crushed grains with water and cooking them on flat stones. These cakes were the forerunners of the unleavened flat breads still popular today in Europe and indigenous tribes the world over.

The development of leavened bread has been attributed to the Egyptians of around 2,3008C. They discovered that a mixture of flour and water, if left uncovered for several days, would bubble and swell, and that if this mixed with fresh dough and allowed to stand a few hours before baking, it yields a light and sweet bread. This process of the Egyptians continues today around the world, as a small quantity of raised dough set aside before baking as "starter", can then replicate this process a few days later in the next batch of dough.

Natural leavening remained the basis of western bread baking for 4,200 years and is the basis of western diet bread making. In Rome of the 2nd century BC, there were large public bakeries equipped with mechanical mixers and kneaders driven by animal power.

Much of the art of baking was lost during Europe's "Dark Ages" (5th through 13th centuries) but, by the late medieval times, the baker was once again a highly skilled and trained craftsman. Naturally leavened dough is a living thing and to control it under varying conditions, to turn out a consistent product day after day, is an acquired fine art. It took a long apprenticeship in those days and now for a successful product.

In the middle of the last century a major change occurred. The work of scientists like Justus von Liebig (the founder of modern nutritional science) and Louis Pasteur led to the discovery and identification of microorganisms that are responsible for the fermentation process. One of these, the single cell yeast species *saccharomyces cerevisiae*, was isolated and cultured. Used by itself it was found to cause a very rapid, uniform, and predictable raising of dough, thus yeast bread was born.

The phenomenon of leavening is based on several facts. One is that the air contains a variety of microorganisms, such as fungi and molds. Another is that when introduced to a proper host, and conditions of proper moisture and humidity are correct, they will initiate fermentation, of which one aspect is the breaking down of complex carbohydrate molecules into simpler sugars or monosaccharides, with the release of carbon dioxide.

Some three quarters of the grain consumption of Americans is in using wheat and wheat flour. For human survival in the future, spelt is an ecologically ideal grain. The spelt kernel is not a hybrid like wheat. Spelt of the labeled common spelt is useable for planting, sprouting, etc. Spelt requires a minimum of care. It will germinate (the common variety) unlike hybrid grains and plants whose don't reproduce. Spelt grows in a variety of climates. Due to its inborn resistance, it is not susceptible to typical grain diseases. The spelt kernel is tightly encased in a strong hull which protects the grain from smog pollution and radiation from space or from man based experiments or naturally occurring elements in the earth. The hulls must be removed with a de-hulling machine of which farmers utilize. The hulls make excellent material as insulation in homes and work areas. Spelt is an excellent seed for storage purposes and far superior in nutrition than most other grains, especially wheat.

After searching for my own grain source to bake with, I found Ridzon Farms. Bob Ridzon runs the farm with his brother (?). The founder of the farm was Leonard Ridzon who was a commercial grower and author of two books, The Carbon Connection and Carbon Cycle. Both books are still available. Leonard has passed on but his integrity for the best spelt and other quality crops and seed is continued through both his sons who I call when I need some grain or corn delivered anywhere in the US.

Quoting Leonard about spelt: "There are four environmental varieties of spelt currently to my knowledge in the United States. They are: one is common, which is what we've got; the other one is called Champ; the third variety is Vita; and then the newest one, which was brought in from Luxemburg, now you have to keep in mind the Luxemburg model, to my knowledge was originally obtained from Germany. Those are the four kinds to my knowledge in the United States. The only one that will grow toxic free is the common spelt. The original common spelt came from Germany back in the early 1800's. The German variety is the result of the changing of soils in the early 1900's in Germany where spelt is called Dinkle, and that was a complete transformation of the energy fields in the soil to negative energy or an over acid condition. Dinkle is Vita spelt from Germany and has a darker bronze color than the Champ does. Common spelt is a light beige color with stronger sprouting seeds that produce a consistent crop from each generation of seed to the next crop.

Yes, the Common originally came from Germany years ago in the 1800's they brought the seed with them. It's been planted here ever since. There is also evidence of the tenth century usage in Europe by Hildegard of Bingham. Spelt has also been recorded eaten as long as 9,000 years ago which makes common spelt an ancient grain indeed.

The percentage of protein in spelt grain should run between 12-15% on the finished product. When it goes over that then it becomes toxic and the molds will grow on the bread and all the things happen that tell you that toxic conditions are present. One of the methods of testing off afflitoxins and micro toxins is molds, and they use 5 molds for that testing by the scientific community." Said Leonard aidzon in contact newspaper in 1993.

He also recommends to farmers plant rotation: 2 years soy beans then 2 years spelt of the common variety because bacteria in the soil that produced the food for the spelt are completely different than the ones that produce the food for the soybean. The crop determines and stimulates what bacteria grow well. Common spelt gets 98% of its nutrients directly from the air and only 2% from the ground leaving the soil. Bacteria and nutrient percentages are higher over yearly farming taxing the soil less and will keep it healthy longer.

Spelt has less gluten than wheat even though the spelt flour is a little sweeter than wheat and far more nourishing.

Very important! The information contained in this book is intended for educational and research purposes only. It is not provided in order to diagnose, prescribe, or treat any disease. The author, publisher, printers, and distributors accept no responsibility for such use. Any individual suffering from any disease, illness, or injury should consult with their physician.

Analysis

Spelt contains all of the basic materials for a healthy body, including Protein, fats, carbohydrates, vitamins, trace elements, and minerals. It also contains vital growth and cell nutritive substances (viridine) which until now have not been isolated, as well as assimilation factor, not identified at this time.

Vita-Spelt Noodles
100% Whole Grain Spelt Flour

	Average per 100 grams	Average per serving 2oz=56.7g	Nutritional information per serving
Moisture, grams	6.62	3.73	
Calories	382.00	216.59	220
Protein, grams	14.26	8.09	10
Ash, grams	1.67	0.95	
Fat, total grams	2.94	1.67	2
Carbohydrate, grams	74.51	42.25	42
Potassium, mg	385.00	218.30	220
Sodium, mg	1.72	0.98	0
Vitamin A, IU	41.0	23.25	*
Vitamin C, mg	0.0	0.00	*
Thiamine, mg	0.649	0.37	25
Riboflavin, mg	0.2	27	0.13 8
Niacin, mg	8.46	4.80	25
Calcium, mg	6.96	3.95	*
Iron, mg	4.17	2.36	15

Percentage of US RDA
   * Contains less than 2 percent of the US RDA of these Nutrients

Spelt is a high protein food of the past for the demand of the future. The total protein content of spelt varies from 13.1-14.28% depending on climate and soil conditions. It is higher than soft wheat (10.5%) and spring wheat (9.1%) but similar to durum wheat (13.8%). The sequence of amino acids also differs between spelt and wheat, spelt containing more cystine, isoleucine, methionine, and neurotransmitters, phenylalaine and tryptophane.

A comparison of amino acids between WHEAT and SPELT is shown below:

Amino Acids mg/g fresh weight	Wheat	Spelt
Cystine	1.10	1.35
Isoleucine	4.40	5.60
Leucine	6.00	9.00
Methionine	2.40	4.00
Phenylalaine	5.00	7.00
Threonine	5.50	5.60
Lysine	2.90	2.75
Tryptophane	1.20	1.80
Valine	4.20	5.80

In comparison with other grains spelt has generally more vitamins and basic minerals. Therefore Hildegard's saying: "spelt is the very best grain" is true.

Average mg per 100 grams	Barley	Rye	Wheat	Oats	Spelt
Vitamin B1	0.43	0.35	0.48	0.52	0.649
Vitamin B2	0.18	0.17	0.14	0.17	0.227
Potassium	-	-	481.00	335.00	385.00
Calcium	38.00	115.00	43.70	79.60	38.00
Iron	2.80	5.10	3.30	5.80	4.17
Manganese	1.70	2.40	2.40	3.70	2.90
Copper	0.30	0.50	0.44	0.47	0.62
Zinc	2.70	1.30	3.36	4.00	3.40

Sources: product analyses souci, milupa (11.11.88) and SCI-TEK Lab.

Spelt is rich in polyunsaturated fats and contains no cholesterol. Polyunsaturated fats or essential fatty acids, which cannot be produced by the body, are nevertheless necessary for body functions. Linoleic acid (26.8%) and oleic acid (26.4% in spelt) are particularly responsible for lubricating the nerve cells. The total fat content of spelt is 2% and can be analyzed as follows:

C8	caprylic acid	0.2%
C10	caprinic acid	0.1%
C12	laurinic acid	0.057
C14	rnyristinic acid	0.1%
C14'	myristoleinic acid	0.2%
C16	palmitic acid	30.0%
C16'	palmi toleinic acid	0.1%
C18	stearic acid	2.4°/a
C18'	oleic acid	2.4%
C18"	linoleic acid	26.4%
C20"	arachinic acid	26.8%
C20"	eicosadienic acid	0
C20"	arachidonic acid	16%
C22	behenic acid	0
C22'	eurainic acid	0.2%
C24	lignocerinic acid	1.0%
C24'	nervonic acid	2.87

Trace Analysis

Almost every food grown today contains chemicals which create cancer in animal experiments and can often be carcinogenic in human beings as well. These chemicals are found in pesticides, herbicides, and insecticides, such as DDT, which, even in small amounts taken orally with foods tat have been sprayed, encourage the growth of tumors. Traces of heavy metals like lead, cadmium, mercury, and arsenic are also hazardous to health and can be found in all conventionally grown foods. Organically grown spelt contains none of these detriments. To the contrary, it grows in the poorest soil in high altitudes without intensive fertilization. Through its husk spelt is even protected from radioactive fallout as could be observed during the Chernobyl catastrophe in 1986.

Saint Hildegard of Bingen, a German mystic of the twelfth century left behind a wealth of knowledge about the body and spirit of an individual that uses the four-element system and the four-humor system dating even further back to the time of the ancient systems of ayurveda, the traditional medicine of India. Hildegard's insights into the spiritual knowledge and its relationship to the mind and body are valuable and still can be used today. Her views on nutrition as natural medicine balanced with spiritual applications first written in the twelfth century middle Latin language, later translated into German, later to become translated into twentieth century English.

Hildegord was primarily a mystic concerned with our relationship to spiritual matters and the divine. Hildegard produced all her works, as she indicated through her heavenly or spiritual vision about her herbal and dietary systems. She advocates the many benefits of whole grain spelt in ones diet bringing balance back to the human system.

It is noted that no health claims are herein made, nor is the publisher, writer, and/or distributor responsible for the application of any material in this book. There is no substitution for consultation, diagnosis, and/or treatment by a licensed physician or other health care professional. Consult your physician on matters of health.

This book is intended for the purpose of baking fine bread and cakes that anyone who desires can learn to create. Hildegard of Bingen used spelt in many of her diet formulas, I mention this reference for interested parties toward research. Please refer to Bear & Company, ci book publisher, about Hildegard and Gottfried Hertzka MD (Folk Wisdom series) for much more insight into Hildegard's remedies and wisdom.

Using Different Flours

Many flours have varied qualities creating different textures and tastes, also gluten content which can assist the rising process of dough. Nutritional content is also important to consider.

♦ **All purpose flour:** is generally refined wheat flour that is lower in gluten content than bread flour. It is used in quick bread recipes and yeast breads made by hand but it can also be a combination of flours made into a bakers blend.

♦ **Bread flour:** is wheat flour made from high gluten wheat. This higher gluten content of bread flour makes it ideal for bread machine use. However the bran and germ have been removed from bread flour, and some brands are bleached and bromoted—a chemical treatment to condition flour to handle the rigorous processing of heavy machines. This is not my flour of choice with these recipes in this books although some brands like Pillsbury bread flour yields consistently good results.

♦ **Whole wheat bread flour:** is whole wheat flour that s ground from hard red spring or winter wheat flours, and is higher in gluten than most whole wheat flours. If you use whole wheat bread flour in your bread machine rather than regular whole wheat flour it will make breads that rise well even though they 100% whole grain.

♦ **Whole wheat all purpose flour:** is a whole wheat flour that is lower in gluten than whole wheat bread flour, and is generally used in quick breads.

♦ **White whole wheat flour:** is milled from hard white wheat. It is lighter in flavor and color than whole wheat flour so offer a more refined gentle quality and makes excellent bread.

♦ **Gluten flour:** is a refined wheat flour that is about 40 to 50% gluten. It is very high in protein and good for hypoglycemics. It is often used to fix low quality flours to increase gluten content to recipes. About 1/4 cup of gluten flour and 3/4 cup of other flour for each cup of flour called for is a general standard.

♦ **Whole spelt flour:** of which there are four different kinds earlier mentioned in this book, is similar to wheat but is higher in gluten and makes marvelous bread and is superior nutritionally. Spelt flours can very as to their baking consistencies from bag to bag. I have found in my experience that common spelt from Ridzon Farms has excellent results and is my flour of choice. Purity Foods spelt flour is also good, milled from another European strain that is higher in protein and gluten than most spelt, and all of the flour is organic as is Ridzon Farms.

♦ **White spelt flour:** is whole spelt flour that has been sifted, removing the fibrous elements of the grain, but not bleached, bromated, or enriched like refined wheat flour usually is, and is available from Purity Foods.

♦ **Barley flour:** is a low gluten flour with a fragile structure when used exclusively and may collapse during baking even if it rises at first.

♦ **Oat flour:** is also a low gluten flour and is an excellent source of soluble fiber but personally I use it with other flours to assist its low gluten content. Oat flour may be harder to digest with those of a weaker intestinal constitution.

♦ **Soy flour:** is ground from soy beans. It is very high in protein and can work to increase protein in other breads.

♦ **Kamut flour:** is another grain flour closely related to wheat although the gluten structure formed is not as strong as wheat's structure. It works well in breads and has a golden yellow color, requires less rising time than wheat but is similar in flavor.

♦ **Rye flour:** has less gluten than wheat and produces dense but flavorful breads. It is great added with other flours.

♦ **Brown rice flour:** is milled from the whole rice grain and contains the rice polish, bran, and germ. It is a gluten free flour, and is acceptable on celiac diets. Eggs or guar gum can be added to recipes to strengthen the structure of rice flour breads.

♦ **Amaranth flour:** is a non-grain flour that is nutritious and high in protein but is very sticky even after baking and makes a very dense bread. It is best kept refrigerated as it may develop a strong flavor.

♦ **Quinoa flour:** another non-grain flour. quinoa is related to beets and spinach. It is high in protein and calcium and other nutrients. It's flavor is very distinct and is best in breads that contain fruit. Quinoa is also dense.

♦ **Buckwheat flour:** is a non-grain flour ground from buckwheat groats, the dark variety is groats that have been roasted.

Wheat Substitutes

Many people are allergic to wheat in any form. As a substitute for 1 cup of wheat flour here are some suggestions:

1 cup spelt flour
1 cup corn flour
3/4 cup coarse cornmeal
1 cup fine cornmeal
1-1/4 cups rye flour
1-1/3 cups oat flour
7/8 cup rice flour
7/8 cup potato starch flour
1 cup soy flour

When substituting for wheat flour, a product of better flavor and texture is obtained by a combination of flours rather than using a single one.

Warmth is most important for yeast to fulfill its purpose. Between 120° and 130° which is higher than most bakers agree the norm calls for 100° to 120° in conventional recipes. I recommend using a kitchen thermometer to measure water temperature. It should be hot to the touch for active yeast.

Sweeteners

All sweeteners contain some form of sugar, some are more complex than others which translates into how quickly or not the body processes these substances in the blood stream. The more complex the sweetener, the more slowly the body absorbs it due to containing more nutrients especially in these less refined sweeteners.

- **Barley malt syrup:** sprouted roasted barley, good source of nutrients, more than other sugars.
- **Brown sugar:** white sugar with the addition of molasses
- **Honey:** raw is best, un-pasteurized organic has many minerals and trace elements.
- **Maple Syrup:** less amounts than sugar needed, boiled down tree sap with vitamins and minerals, a little less sweet than honey.
- **Molasses:** a by-product of the sugar refining process contains vitamins and minerals.
- **Rice syrup:** fermented and boiled rice, distinctive flavor.
- **Sucanat:** a pure natural sweetener mode by evaporating the water from sugar cane juice.
- **Turbinado sugar:** raw sugar crystals are washed in a centrifugal, closest to sugar in its natural state, absorbed more slowly by the body.

Sweeteners equal to one cup of turbinado sugar:

1-7/8 cups barley malt syrup	3/4 cup molasses
1-1/8 cups brown sugar	1-7/8 cup rice syrup
3/4 cup honey	1-1/8 cups sucanat
3/4 cup maple syrup	

Yeast & Kneading

Have all ingredients at room temperature when you begin. The addition of two or three ice-cold eggs or butter taken directly from the refrigerator can throw a deep chill into the dough and reduce its ability to produce desired results. A warm bowl is also desired. For the dough the best temperature is between 90° and 100° which is warmer than recommended temperatures. Dough will rise at room temperature also, it will just take longer.

One important difference between working with quick-rising and conventional yeast is that the new quick yeasts should not be proofed. This is a hard habit to break. Grandma did it but today's yeast does not require it. The new yeasts have been designed to be mixed with the flour and not separated out. They do better when sheltered with the other ingredients, which protect them from the high temperatures now recommended (actually all yeasts, conventional as well as quick, should be mixed with the dry ingredients first. Rising times will be reduced greatly by this process. If yeast is to be used infrequently it is better stored in the fridge.

Baking soda: the first chemical leavener to be used, reacts with acids, such as sour cream or buttermilk, to produce carbon dioxide. The reaction is almost instantaneous requiring a fast assembly of ingredients and immediate baking. The main thrust comes from the heat of the oven.

Fat: is a generic term, whether it be butter, lard, margarine, oil, or a combination. Fat imparts richness, softness, and moisture. Fat contributes a unique flavor and also lubricates the gluten in the dough so that it can rise better. Solid vegetable and animal fats are made with oils through which hydrogen gas has been forced under pressure to produce a creamy solid—thus the word hydrogenated. Salad or cooking oil such as olive, safflower, avocado, sesame, sunflower, and grape seed oil are healthy choices. Personally I do not recommend ever using canola or corn oil because of unsafe processing and carcinogenic properties produced by high temperatures.

Salt: controls the action of the yeast in dough and strengthens the gluten. Salt enhances other flavors bringing them out more.

Sugar: imparts a rich brown color through carmelization. In moderate amounts sugar increases yeast fermentation while in high concentrations it will inhibit it.

Milk: a bread loaf made with milk has a browner crust and a velvety grain. The loaf will stay soft longer.

Kneading: gluten, a plant protein found in spelt and more so in wheat flour, forms an elastic webbing to trap the carbon dioxide produced by the yeast. Kneading by hand can be rigorous. Position the arms fully extended so that the height of the work table is more comfortable and palms can rest on the work surface.

    The rough dough is turned out of the bowl onto the work surface which has been sprinkled with flour. If the dough is sticky more flour may be needed. Fold the dough in half, push down hard against it with your hands away from the body. Turn the dough into a quarter turn as you fold and push it each time. Repeat this process of push-turn-fold alternating this pattern frequently by picking up the dough ball above your surface and crashing it down hard. Don't be gentle in the kneading process, vigorous action gives the dough body and suppleness. When fully kneaded the dough will be elastic when pulled apart by the hands stretching the dough.

    If the dough is too firm after the first kneading a little water may be added. If the dough is too soft and slack, add more flour. When dough no longer sticks to hands it has arrived at the proper consistency and is ready to be put aside to rise.

Dough kneaded in a food processor will be slightly sticky when turned out. Just add some sprinkles of flour.

After the dough has doubled in size it is ready for forming into the desired baking size for loaves. Knead each piece to form pan sizes and let rise a second time to double its volume once again. Some old fashioned breads can have three old fashioned breads can have three rising periods.

Dough Volume

Dough volume: determine the total amount of the dough by weight or measure. If the loaf is going to turn out well it must be baked in the proper size pan or baking dish. Too little dough will produce a stunted loaf while too much dough will outgrow the pan.

Pan Size	Inches	Volume	Weight
Large	9x5x3	3 cups	2 pounds
Medium	8x4x2	2-1/2 cups	1-1/2 pounds
Small	7x3x2	1-1/2 cups	1 pound
Miniature	5x3x2	3/4 cup	1/2 pound
Sub-mini	4x2x1	1/2 cup	5 to 6 ounces

Note: depending on the ingredients used variance will be evident to this chart such as heavier grain flours like spelt, whole wheat, rye, bran, and barley flours.

Standard Weights
and Measures

dash	=	8 drops
1 tablespoon	=	3 teaspoons
4 tablespoons	=	¼ cup
5-1/3 tablespoons	=	1/3 cup
8 tablespoons	=	½ cup
16 tablespoons	=	1 cup (dry)
1 fluid ounce	=	2 tablespoons
1 cup liquid	=	½ pint or 8 oz.
2 cups (16oz.)	=	1 pint
2 pints (4 cups)	=	1 quart
4 quarts	=	1 gallon
8 quarts	=	1 peck (dry)
4 pecks	=	1 bushel
16 ounces (dry)	=	1 pound
Herbs, fresh chopped—1 Tbs	=	½ ounce or 15 grams
Nuts, chopped—1 cup	=	5-½ ounce or 155 grams
Raisins—1 Tbs	=	1/3 ounce
Spices, ground—1 tsp	=	1 ½ ounce or 2.5 grams
Spices, ground—2 Tbs	=	½ ounce or 15 grams
Brown sugar—1 Tbs	=	1/3 ounce or 10 grams
Granulated sugar—1 Tbs	=	½ ounce or 15 grams
Confection sugar—1/4 cup	=	1 ounce
Confection sugar—1/2 cup	=	2-¼ ounces
Confection sugar—1 cup	=	4-½ ounces
Butter—1 Tbs	=	½ ounce
Butter—1/2 cup	=	4 ounces

Pastry Pie Crust Chart

Type of Pastry	Flour	Salt	Shortening	Liquid
Basic 1 crust 8"	1 cup sifted all purpose	1/2 tsp	1/3 cup butter or lard	2-1/2 Tbs water
Basic 2 crust 8"	1-1/2 cups sifted all purpose	1 tsp	1/2 cup butter or lard	4 Tbs water
Basic 2 crust 9"	2 cups flour sifted	1-1/2 tsp	2/3 cup butter or lard	5 Tbs water
Basic 2 crust 10"	3 cups flour sifted	1-1/2 tsp	1 cup butter	7-1/2 lbs water
French pastry 1 crust 8 or 9"	2 cups flour sifted	1/2 tsp	1 cup butter	1 Tbs vinegar or 2 lbs lemon juice

French pastry—In step one, add 2 Tbs sugar, 1-1/3 Tbs double acting baking powder, 1 egg, or 2 egg yolks beaten.

Type of Pastry	Flour	Salt	Shortening	Liquid
Quick 2 crust 8 or 9"	2-1/4 cups flour sifted	1 tsp	1/2 cup + 1 Tbs olive oil	1/3 cup cold milk
Almond, pecan, walnut, hazelnut, or macadamia	Same as basic pastry pie crust. In step 1 add 2/3 cup ground nuts			
Whole wheat or spelt 8 or 9"	1-1/2 cups flour	1/2 tsp	1/2 cup butter	1/4 cup ice water
Spelt 2 crust 8 or "	3 cups flour	I tsp	1/4 cup oil 1/4 cup butter	6 Tbs ice water add 1 egg
Graham cracker	1-1/3 cups crumbs	1/3 cup sugar	1/4 cup butter melted	Bake at 350° 15 minutes or line pan and chill

Mixer Breads
Made with high-gluten flours

To make yeast bread using high-gluten such as wheat, spelt, kamut, or rye, with your mixer, put 1/2 to 2/3 of the flour, all of the yeast, salt, and other dry ingredients in the mixer bowl. Mix on low speed for about 30 seconds. Warm the liquid ingredients to 115-120°F. With the mixer on low speed, add the liquids to the dry ingredients in a slow stream. Continue mixing until the dry and liquid ingredients are well mixed.

If your mixer is not a heavy duty mixer, at this point beat the dough for 5 to 10 minutes. Knead the rest of the flour in by hand, kneading for about 10 minutes or until dough is very smooth and elastic. If you wish to add raisins or nuts to the dough, do it during this hand kneading period.

If your mixer is a heavy duty mixer, after the liquids are thoroughly mixed in, with the mixer still running, begin adding the rest of the flour around the edges of the bowl 1/2 cup at a time, mixing well after each addition, until the dough forms a ball and cleans the sides of the bowl. Knead the dough on the speed directed in your mixer manual for 5 to 10 minutes or until dough is very elastic and smooth. Turn the dough onto a floured surface and knead it briefly to check the consistency of the dough, kneading in more flour if necessary. Raisins or nuts should be added to the dough by hand after the mixer is finished kneading it.

Put the dough into an oiled bowl and turn it once so that the top of the dough is also oiled. Cover it with a towel and let rise in a warm (85°F to 90°F) place until it has doubled in size, about 45 minutes to one hour.

Punch the dough down and shape it into loaves or rolls as desired. For loaves use an 8"x4 or 9x5 oiled loaf pan. Allow it to rise until doubled again. Bake at 350° to 375°F usually for 45 minutes to 1 hour for loaves and at 375° for 15 to 23 minutes for rolls.

Mixer Spelt Bread

Yield: 2 loaves

4 cups spelt flour

2 packages (4-1/2 tsp) active dry or quick rise yeast

1-1/4 tsp salt

1/3 cup apple juice warmed to 120°F minutes

1-2/3 cup water at about 120°F

2 Tbs olive oil

1 Tbs liquid lecithin or additional oil

An additional 2-1/4 to 2-3/4 cups spelt flour

Prepare the dough as in the mixer bread directions on preceding page. After the first rise, punch down the dough and shape it into two loaves. Put each loaf into a well oiled loaf pan. Let the loaves rise until they have doubled again, about 45 minutes. Bake at 375° for 40 to 45 minutes. Immediately run a knife around the edges of the loaves and remove from pans. Cool on a wire rack.

Mixer Kamut Bread

Yield: 2 loaves

4 cups kamut flour

2 packages (4-1/2 tsp) active dry

1-1/2 tsp salt

2-1/2 cups water at about 120°F the pans, about 35 to 50 minutes

3 Tbs olive oil or substitute additional 2-1/2 to 3 cups kamut flour

Prepare the dough as in the mixer bread directions except do not let it rise the first time after dough has elastic consistency. Shape into two loaves. Put each loaf into an oiled 8" by 4" pan. Let the loaves rise in a warm place until double or reach the top of the pans, about 35 to 50 minutes. Remove the loaves from the pans immediately. Cool on a wire rack.

Sourdough

Even in its ancient origins, the art of sourdough cookery is still considered complicated and even mysterious by some today. There is no mystery. Sourdough is simply a home-grown yeast factory, discovered by woman and man long after they had learned how to pound roots or grind wild grain into flour. The discovery of sourdough was probably an accident of left over dough kept warm enough to keep the airborn bacteria alive and bubbly. They also learned this sourdough starter could be kept going indefinitely, provided they replenished what was used out of the pot or container with fresh flour and water and kept it at the proper degree of warmth so it would continue to work" or ferment. Too much heat would kill this yeast factory. It would also be rendered dormant by cold although it would be brought back as soon as warmed up to room temperature again, around 70°F.

To show where to begin you're going to learn how to make sourdough starter which takes about a minute to do:

♦ Put 2 cups of flour into a crock, jar, or Tupperware bowl that is at room temperature. Even a glass mason jar works well but never use a metal container.
♦ Add 2-1/2 cups lukewarm water.
♦ Set the whole batch in a warm place, but not too hot of a place.
♦ That's it. In about 4 or 5 days the pot will be bubbling slowly and a distinct aroma will be wafting into the air from it.

Of course you can help it along by adding a package of yeast to it, or you can use warm water that you've just boiled potatoes in as a substitute before using the original warm water. While it is convenient to keep a starter going at all times, provided you use some and replenish what you use with fresh flour and water frequently, it can be kept for several weeks under refrigeration, and frozen even longer. Just remember to always bring it back to room temperature so it becomes active again before using it in recipes

Always sterilize your container first to remove or inhibit the growth of unwanted bacteria. In cold weather, starters lose some potency but can be revived with a tablespoon of pure cider vinegar. A loose fitting cover is desired but never tightly closed because the mixture has to attract those yeast spore from the surrounding air.
Some secrets for good sourdough cooking are:

♦ Avoid mixing the batter too much. Over mixing knocks the gas out of the dough, which is needed for the rising process.
♦ Sourdough cooking requires slightly more heat or a longer cooking time than ordinary baking.
♦ Never put back in the starter pot anything but flour and water.
♦ If starter turns orange, throw it away.
♦ Use lukewarm water, never hot or cold water.
♦ Baking soda turns sourdough yellow, so you may want to use baking powder instead.
♦ Wheat or spelt flour in starter does not rise as high but works faster than white flour.
♦ The batter should always be at room temperature when you use it.
♦ When making starter, first warm the pot or container with hot water.
♦ Buttermilk usually requires a bit more leavening when used in most recipes.
♦ A starter should be used and replenished at least once a week or more often would be better. In between you can keep it in a bowl in the fridge or frozen in the freezer.
♦ When replenishing a starter use warm water and enough flour and let this work in the pot for at least a day before storing it in a refrigerator.
♦ Allow for expansion of the starter mixture in a larger container when going out of town.

Sourdough French Bread
With Wheat or Spelt

1 pack of active dry yeast

1-1/2 cups lukewarm water

1 cup sourdough starter

4 cups flour: spelt, wheat, or other

2 Tbs sugar, honey, or maple syrup

1-1/2 tsp salt

Large bowl 10-12 quarts

1 more cup of flour

1/2 tsp baking soda

1. Dissolve package of yeast in 1-1/2 cups of warm water. Let stand 5 minutes then mix in sourdough starter into bowl adding 4 cups of flour. 2 lbs sugar, and 1-1/2 tsp salt. Cover with a cloth and let rise n a warm place until doubled in size.

2. Mix in a cup of flour and 1/2 tsp baking soda into the dough, adding enough flour to make a stiff dough. Knead on a flour dusted board until smooth and shiny. Knead well, about 10-12 minutes.

3. Shape the dough into half loaf sizes. Place on greased paper or sheet pan sprinkled with corn meal. Leave in a warm place until doubled in size.

4. Brush the top lightly with cold water, Make a sharp slash about 1/4 inch deep in top of loaf. Bake in a 400°F oven. Place a shallow pan with a little hot water on the oven bottom. Bake until dark almond brown. Brush with melted butter and hot water. Crisp in the oven for 3 to 5 minutes. (Note: it helps to use a bit of salad oil on your hands before kneading dough.)

5. Allow to cool for 7 to 10 minutes before serving.

Sourdough French Bread II

1 package of active dry yeast

1-1/4 cups warm water

1/2 cup milk

2 Tbs olive oil

2 tsp salt

2 Tbs sugar or other sweetener

4-1/2 cups un-sifted flour, either wheat, spelt, all purpose or a mixture of rye, buckwheat, spelt, or wheat

1/4 cup sourdough starter

1. Dissolve package of yeast into 1/4 cup of warm water, let stand 5 minutes. Combine this with 4-1/2 cups un-sifted flour. 2 Tbs sugar, 2 tsp salt, 1 cup water, 1/2 cup milk, 2 Tbs olive oil, and 1/4 cup sourdough starter. Mix well.

2. Knead lightly and place in greased bowl to rise until doubled.

3. Turn out onto floored board and divide in two parts. Shape dough in oblongs and then roll up tightly, beginning with one side. Seal outside edge by pinching and shape into size wanted. Place loaves on greased baking sheet and let rise until doubled again.

4. Slash diagonal cuts on top with a knife and brush with water. Bake at 400°F for about 25 minutes.

5. Allow to cool for 6-7 minutes before eating, cool 25 minutes before refrigerating or freezing.

Sourdough Banana Bread

1/3 cup shortening or soft butter

1 cup sugar

1 egg

1 cup mashed banana

1 cup sourdough starter

2 cups spelt or desired flour

1 tsp salt

1 tsp baking powder

1 tsp baking soda

3/4 cup chopped walnuts

1 tsp vanilla

1 tsp grated orange rind

1. Cream together the butter or shortening, sugar and egg, mix well. Stir in bananas and sourdough starter. Add orange rind and vanilla. Sift flour, measure again with salt, baking powder, and baking soda. Add flour mixture to the first mixture, stirring just until blended.

2. Pour into greased 9x5 inch loaf pan. Bake in oven at 350°F for 1 hour or until toothpick comes out clean.

3. Cool before slicing.

Exceptional Handmade Spelt Whole Grain Bread

Yield: 5 loaves

4 1/4oz packages of dry yeast

1/2 blackstrap molasses

3-1/4 cups warm water

1-1/2 tsp salt

9 eggs beaten

1/2 cup honey

1/2 cup dark brown sugar (optional)

2 tsp baking soda

2-1/2 Tbs vanilla extract

12 to 14 cups fresh ground spelt flour

1-1/4 Lbs melted butter

3 Tbs olive oil

1. Using an 8qt bowl, add 1 cup warm water to active dry yeast and let stand 5-6 minutes.
2. Add honey, sugar, and salt. Stir well. Add beaten eggs, molasses, and olive oil. Add remaining water, mix well.
3. In a separate bowl mix baking powder and baking soda into 4 cups spelt flour. Add melted butter. Add to main bowl mixture. Add vanilla extract.
4. Whisk in more flour one cup at a time until dough thickens then knead by hand, adding remaining flour into bowl or on a floured surface until dough is elastic and firm without sticking to surface or hands.
5. Cover with a towel. Let rise 1-1/3 hours in a warm place 70-80°F in a large sheet pan.
6. When dough is doubled punch down and divide into 5 equal balls. Knead each ball well, about 5-6 minutes more and shape into loaves.
7. Grease pans with olive oil and place loaves in them. Let rise 10 minutes then bake at 325°F about 1 hour, turning pans once half way through baking time. Insert toothpick or knife into one loaf, if it comes out clean remove bread from oven.

Buttermilk Biscuits

Yield: 12 each

Note: recipe may be doubled or tripled.

2 cups flour

1/2 tsp salt

2 tsp baking powder

1/2 tsp baking soda

1 tsp sugar

1/2 cup butter, room temperature

2/3 cup buttermilk

Additions:

1   cup cheddar cheese, 1/4 cup diced green onions, and 1/4 tsp fresh ground black pepper for a festive flavor.

1. Mix dry ingredients first. Add room temperature butter then buttermilk and lightly stiff with fork

2. Knead dough on floured surface by pushing down then folding then turning dough 10-12 times.

3. Roll out until 1/2 inch thick in a large square. Cut with cup or biscuit cutter to desired size.

4. Place on greased baking sheet and set in a warm place to rise for 15 minutes.

5. Bake at 400°F for 12-15 minutes until a light golden brown.

French Bread for Baguettes

Yield: 2 long 15" baguettes

2 eggs beaten well

3 to 3-1/2 cups bread flour (or 1-1/2 cups spelt and 1-3/4 cups other bread flour)

1 package active dry yeast

1 Tbs sugar

1 tsp salt

1 cup hot water (120° to 130°F)

2 Tbs soft butter

2 baguette pans or one long baking sheet pan well greased and lightly sprinkled with corn meal

1. Measure 2-1/2 cups of flour into a mixing or mixer bowl and add the yeast, sugar, and salt. Pour in the hot water and melted butter. Beat with a wooden spoon or for 2 minutes with the mixer flat beater, it takes a little longer by hand. Add remaining flour 1/4 cup at a time until mixture is no longer moist but soft and elastic. Lift the dough from the bowl and place on a lightly floured surface, or if in an electric mixer, attach the dough hook.

2. Knead the dough by hand with a push-turn-fold rhythm, adding sprinkles of flour if the dough is too moist or sticky. Occasionally lift the dough.above the work surface and bring it crashing down to help the gluten work. If in a mixer add more sprinkles of flour if the dough persists in sticking to sides of bowl. Knead for 10 minutes.

3. Place the dough in a greased bowl, cover tightly with plastic wrap, and put aside to rise in a warm place until double in bulk, about 1 hour.

4. Divide the dough into equal parts and roll each under into a 15" long baguette. Lay the dough in or on the pan separated so they won't touch during rising and baking.

5. Second rising—brush loaves with melted butter or olive oil, let rise uncovered until doubled again, about 1 hour.

6. Preheat the oven to 350°F 20 minutes before baking. Place an empty pan on the bottom of the oven or lower rack. Five minutes

before baking pour 1 cup hot water into the pan to create steam for a crispy crust. Warning: be careful not to burn yourself with steam.

7. Bake in the oven for 30 to 40 minutes or until the crust is golden brown. Turn one loaf over and thump with the forefinger to make certain it sounds hard and hollow. (If using a convection oven reduce heat 40°). Remove loaves after baking and place on a wire rack to cool.

Note: tops of bread before baking may be brushed with stiffly beaten egg whites and sprinkled with sesame or poppy seeds.

Homemade Pizza (Spelt) Pizzetta

Yield: two 10" pizzas

1/4oz dry yeast (1 package)

1-1/2 cups warm water 80°-85°F

4-1/2 cups spelt flour

1 tsp salt

2 Tbs extra virgin olive oil

1. To begin the dough place the yeast and 1/2 cup warm water in a mixing bowl and set aside for 10 minutes. Stir in the remaining water and one cup flour. Add the salt and olive oil, stir. Add the remaining flour 1 cup at a time, mixing each thoroughly before adding the next until you have just 1/2 cup left.

2. Turn the dough out onto a floured surface and knead until it is smooth and velvety, about 7 minutes, working in as much of the remaining flour as the dough will take. Place the dough in a clean bowl well coated with olive oil. Cover with a damp towel, set in a warm place 800 to 90°F and let rise 2 hours.

3. Punch the dough down, let it rise 5 minutes and form it into two 10 inch pizza shells. Let the dough rest on baking sheets or pizza stones for 5 to 7 minutes. You are now ready for your favorite toppings.

Suggestions: coat the pizza shells with olive oil and garlic, roasted vegetables and cheese, or any red sauce with herbs basil, oregano, parsley, mozzarella, parmesan, fontina and cheeses. Or spread shells with olive oil, sprinkle dill and parsley. Top with mushrooms, smoked salmon, capers, and goat cheese with diced tomatoes and green or red onions chopped fine. Yuuummm.

Lemon Apricot Cookies

Yield; 3 dozen

3/4 cup blanched, slivered almonds, toasted arid diced

2/3 cup powdered sugar, divided

2 cups minus 2 Tbs flour

3 Tbs finely grated lemon zest

1/4 tsp salt

1 cup (2 sticks) butter softened

2 Tbs water

2 tsp vanilla extract

1 tsp lemon extract

1/3 cup chopped dried apricots

Granulated sugar (for coating)

1. Place 1/4 cup almonds and 1 Tbs powdered sugar in food processor or blender, cover and process until nuts are powder fine. Chop remaining 1/2 cup almonds arid set aside.

2. In a medium bowl whisk together flour, powder fine almonds, lemon zest, and salt. In a large mixer bowl cream butter and remaining powdered sugar until light and fluffy. Beat in water and extracts until well blended. On low speed gradually beat in flour.

3. Stir in apricots and chopped almonds. Refrigerate dough covered for 2 hours until firm. Briefly knead dough until it can be shaped. Measure dough by level tablespoon and roll into 1 inch balls, coat well with granulated sugar. Place balls two inches apart on ungreased cookie sheets. Using a flat-bottom glass press each ball into two inch rounds.

4. Bake in a preheated 375°F oven for 10-12 minutes or just until areIy brown around edges. Remove and cool completely on wire racks. Store in tightly covered container for 1 week, or freeze for 2 months.

Spelt Sesame Tahini Bread

Yield: 12 squares 4"x4"

2 ripe bananas

1/2 tsp salt

3/4 Lb butter (room temperature)

16 ounces tahini (sesame seed paste)

2 cups honey

2 cups brown sugar

2 Tbs vanilla extract

1-1/2 tsp baking powder

1 tsp baking soda

1-1/2 tsp ginger (ground)

1/4 tsp nutmeg (ground)

1 Tbs sesame oil

6 cups spelt flour

12"x17" baking sheet pan with 3/4" sides

1. In a large bowl cream bananas, then add egg and whip well. Add sugar and tahini paste, then oil, honey, vanilla, and melted butter. Mix well.

2. Mix in two cups of flour with salt, baking powder, baking soda, ginger, and nutmeg. Add two more cups of flour then the last two cups gradually.

3. Pour into well greased baking sheet and bake in a preheated oven at 325° on the middle rack.

Lemon Spice Quick Bread

Yield: one 1 pound loaf

1 cup whole grain spelt flour

3/4 cup barley flour

1 Tbs aluminum free baking powder

1/4 cup butter

1/4 cup honey or brown sugar

I tsp fresh lemon rind

1/2 cup rice syrup

1/2 tsp vanilla extract

Pinch of ground cinnamon

Pinch of ground cloves

2 eggs separated

1 cup of water

2 Tbs fresh lemon juice

1. Preheat oven to 350°F. Lightly coat a 1 pound loaf pan with olive oil, set aside.
2. Sift all flours with baking powder in a 2 quart bowl, set aside.
3. Place butter in another 2 quart bowl and cream it with the lemon rind, rice syrup, vanilla, and spices. Mix thoroughly. Add egg yolks and mix well.
4. Combine water and lemon juice in a 3 quart bowl. Regin beating the lemon mixture with a wooden spoon, continue beating as you add flour and butter mixture. Mix well.
5. Place egg whites in a 1 quart bowl and beat with an electric mixer until they form stiff peaks. Gently fold whites into batter.
6. Spoon the batter info the prepared pan and bake for 45 to 60 minutes, or until toothpick in the center of the loaf comes out clean. Allow to cool in pan for 10 minutes before removing to a wire rack. Cool completely before slicing.

American Indian Bread

Yield: two 1 pound loaves

1 cup warm water, divided

1 package (1/4 oz) active dry yeast

2 Tbs turbinado, brown sugar, or honey

1 cup buttermilk

1/4 cup butter

1/2 cup blackstrap molasses

1-1/2 tsp salt

4 cups whole grain spelt flour

1 cup rye flour

Egg glaze:

1 egg white

2 Tbs milk

1. Place 1/4 cup of warm water in a 1 quart bowl, stir in yeast and sugar, set aside.
2. Warm up buttermilk in a sauce pan, add butter, the remaining warm water, molasses, and salt.
3. Combine the buttermilk mixture and yeast mixture in a 3 quart bowl. Add half of the flour and beat well. Cover and let rise for 30 minutes.
4. Mix the remaining flour into the dough a half cup at a time until the dough pulls away from the sides of the bowl without sticking. Turn dough onto a lightly floured board and knead for 5 minutes or until dough is smooth and elastic.
5. Clean the 3 quart bowl and coat with olive or safflower oil. Return dough to bowl, cover and let rise in a warm place 2 hours.
6. Punch the dough down, turn out and knead for 3 minutes. Divide the dough in half and shape each piece into a round ball.
7. Coat two 8 inch round baking pans with oil and sprinkle with cornmeal. Place dough into each pan and let rise for 1 hour.
8. Preheat over to 375°F. Make the egg glaze, place egg white and milk in a 1 quart bowl, beat well.
9. Bake 40 minutes or until nicely browned. Allow loaves to cool before removing.

Raisin Bread

Yield: four 1 pound loaves

15 ounces dark raisins

1 cup apple juice

2-3 packages 1/4oz each active dry yeast

1/2 cup warm water

3/4 cup butter room temperature

2 Tbs olive oil

1 cup turbinado or brown sugar

I tsp cinnamon

I tsp sea salt

2 tsp grated fresh lemon peel

2 tsp almond extract

5 cups low fat milk or substitute liquid

5 cups sifted white spelt flour

5 cups whole grain spelt flour

4 eggs well beaten

1/2 cup blackstrap molasses

1. Place raisins and apple juice in a 2 quart bowl. Cover bowl and allow to soak overnight. The next day drain and discard the apple juice, keep the raisins.
2. Place yeast in warm water in a 1 quart glass bowl, stir and set aside for 5 to 10 minutes.
3. Place the butter, sugar, lemon peel, almond extract, and molasses in a 3 quart bowl and cream together.
4. Warm milk but do not boil.
5. Pour hot milk over raisins. Add to butter mixture and stir well.
6. Mix both flours well in a 3 quart bowl. Add 2 cups of flour to the butter mixture. Mix for 2 minutes.
7. Add yeast mixture to the bowl and blend. Stir in half of the remaining flour 1/2 cup at a time. Mix eggs in with dough.
8. Turn dough onto a lightly floured surface, knead about 3 minutes adding additional flour if dough is too sticky. Grease a 5 quart bowl with olive oil. Form dough into a large smooth ball and place in bowl. Cover with towel or plastic wrap and place in a warm place to rise for 2 hours or until doubled.

9. Punch the dough down, divide into 4 equal pieces and form each piece into a loaf. Oil pans before placing dough in them. Cover pans and let rise about 2 hours more in a warm place until doubled in size.

10. Preheat over to 375°F, bake loaves for 50 minutes or until they Sound hollow when tapped. Let loaves cool before removing from pans.

Wholegrain Spelt Bread II

Made Easy

Yield 1 round loaf

1-1/2 cups whole grain spelt flour

2 packages (1/4oz each) active dry yeast

A pinch of salt

1 cup plain yogurt

1/2 cup club soda

1/4 cup honey

2 Tbs melted butter or olive oil

1 egg beaten

14/3 cups spelt flour

1. Combine 1-1/2 cups of spelt flour with yeast and salt in a 3 quart bowl. Mix lightly and let stand 5 to 6 minutes.

2. Combine the yogurt, club soda, honey, and olive oil or melted butter in a 2 quart sauce pan. Place over medium heat, cook until warm but not hot to the touch (do not boil).

3. Add the yogurt mixture to the flour mixture and stir together. Add egg and mix the ingredients with an electric mixer on low speed until the dry ingredients are moistened. Increase the speed and beat 3 more minutes. Add remaining 1-1/2 cup flour and mix thoroughly.

4. Coat 1-1/2 quart round casserole dish or bread pan with olive oil. Pour batter into dish. Cover with a towel and let rise 1 to 1-1/2 hours or until the dough rises to the top of the dish.

5. Preheat oven to 375°F. Bake the loaf for 35 to 40 minutes or until golden in color. Allow 5 minutes to cool in dish before removing. Serve warm or toasted.

Spelt Buns—Whole Grain

Yield: 20 buns

3-1/2 cups warm water

3 packages (1/4oz each) active dry yeast

3 eggs

1/2 tsp baking soda

1 tsp salt

1/3 cup lecithin or melted butter

1/3 cup olive oil

1/3 cup honey

11 cups whole grain spelt flour

2 Tbs molasses

1. Place 1/2 cup of water in a 1 quart bowl and sprinkle with the yeast. Stir a few times and set aside for 5 to 10 minutes.

2. Combine the remaining 3 cups of water, eggs, baking soda, salt, butter, honey, and molasses in a 3 quart bowl. Add 4 cups of the flour and mix thoroughly. Set aside for 15 minutes.

3. Add the yeast mixture to the other bowl of ingredients, mix well. Add enough of remaining flour to make a stiff dough.

4. Turn the dough onto a lightly floured board and knead for 10 minutes, or until the dough is smooth and elastic. Cover dough with a towel and let rise on a board in a warm place until doubled in size.

5. Push down dough and divide into 20 equal sized pieces. Arrange the pieces on the board, spacing them one inch apart. Let dough rest for 10 minutes.

6. Lightly coat two 17x11 inch cookie sheets with salad or olive oil. Using floured hands, shape the dough into burns on the cookie sheet pans, spacing them about 2 inches apart. Cover buns with a towel and let rise for 45 minutes to 1 hour, or when buns double in size.

7. Preheat oven to 425°F. Brush melted butter or olive oil on buns and bake for about 15 minutes or until golden brown. Allow buns to cool for 5 minutes.

Crepes

25 each	12 each (1/2 batch)
2-1/4 cups sifted spelt flour	1-1/8 cups flour
2 oz. butter melted	1 oz. butter melted
1 Tbs brown sugar	2 tsp brown sugar
1/4 tsp salt	1 pinch of salt
4 cups whole milk	2 cups whole milk
8 eggs	4 eggs
1 Ths olive oil	1 Tbs olive oil

1. Whip eggs in a large bowl. Add sugar and salt, mix well. Add one half of the milk and whip into egg mixture. Slowly add flour mixing well until blended. Add remaining milk and whip well.
2. Pour batter through wire mesh double strainer to remove any flour lumps that did not blend. Whip in warm butter. Cover and chill batter two hours in a pitcher or tall container with a pour spout or small opening.
3. Using one or two burners at the same time—electric or gas on medium heat or flame—coot two 12 inch nonstick skillets using a paper towel folded with olive oil, when pans are warm enough. Pour approximately I-1/2oz. Of batter by eye into raised pan held up parallel with stove top, with crepe batter in right hand and pan in left hand. Immediately after pouring batter into pan, rotate pan in a tilted semi-circle to coat entire bottom of pan to spread out batter. Note: the batter starts to cook immediately so you have to work fast. After even thickness of coating across pan, return pan to stove burner to cook until edges of crepe turn golden brown, about 45 to 60 seconds. Crepe is now ready to flip. Carefully pull up one edge of crepe circle with a wooden spoon or a heat tempered rubber spatula. Brown on second side about 15 seconds. Fold crepe out of pan onto wax paper by turning pan

upside down over wax paper. Be gentle for crepes are very fragile, Alternate pouring batter into pans—one, then second pan about 1 minute apart to speed the process. This way working two crepes at a time alternating pans and flipping procedure. After the first few crepes you will get the hang of it. If a crepe tears don't despair—they still taste great.

Filling suggestions:

1. Mixed fruit—warm or cold with nuts
2. Sautéed vegetables with olive oil and basil pesto
3. Cooked chicken, spices, cheese, salsa, sour cream
4, Smoked salmon, capers, red onion, tomato, herbs
5. Fresh wilted spinach, onion, mushroom, jack cheese
6. Just top with powdered sugar or chocolate sauce
7. Sautéed apple slices, raisins, cinnamon, sugar, and vanilla ice cream
8. Scrambled eggs with any favorite vegetable or meat and cheese topped with sour cream or salsa
9. Try your own ideas

Cherry Cobbler

Yield: 6 servings

2 cups canned pitted cherries (reserve juice)

1 Tbs quick tapioca

1/3 cup granulated sugar

1/8 tsp salt

3/4 cup cherry juice

1/2 tsp almond or vanilla extract

1 Tbs lemon juice

Topping:

1-1/4 cups sifted flour

1-1/2 tsp double acting baking powder

1/2 tsp salt

2 Tbs sugar

1/4 cup butter

1/4 cup finely chopped almonds or pecans

1/2 cup milk

1. Preheat oven to 400°F. Grease 8 inch square pan.
2. Place cherries in prepared pan. Sprinkle tapioca over cherries.
3. Combine sugar, salt, cherry juice, extract, and lemon juice. Pour over cherries.

Topping:
1. In a small bowl mix and sift flour, baking powder, salt, and sugar together.
2. Slice small flat pieces of butter into flour mixture until surface is well mixed with the consistency of small grain. Add nuts, mix well. Add milk, mix thoroughly with fork.
3. Drop by tablespoonfuls onto cherry mixture. A design may be formed by spacing the dough uniformly in rows.
4. Bake at 400°F for 15 minutes, reduce heat to 350°F and bake for 20 minutes more. Serve plain or topped with vanilla sauce or ice cream.

Berry or Fruit Crisp

Yield: 8 servings

4-1/2 cups peeled, thinly sliced apples, peaches, or pears; or berries or cherries

4 Tbs. lemon juice

4 Tbs. brown sugar

1 cup sifted flour

1 cup packed brown sugar

1 cup quick oats or granola

1/2 tsp salt

1 tsp ground cinnamon

1/3 tsp nutmeg

1/2 tsp ground ginger

1 tsp baking powder

1 cup butter or shortening

1. Preheat oven to 370°F. Grease 20x12x2 inch baking pan.
2. Place fruit or berries in bottom of prepared pan. Sprinkle with lemon Juice and 4 Tbs. brown sugar.
3. In mixing bowl, combine flour, 1 cup brown sugar, oats or granola, salt, cinnamon, nutmeg, ginger, and baking powder. With fork mix in butter. Sprinkle crumbly mixture over fruit.
4. Bake for about 25 minutes until lightly golden brown. Serve hot or cold with ice cream.

Whole Grain Spelt Banana Bread

1/2 cup shortening or soft butter

1 cup brown sugar

3 ripe bananas

2 eggs beaten

2 cups spelt flour

1/2 tsp salt

I tsp baking soda

1 tsp baking powder

1/2 cup chopped nuts

1/2 tsp cinnamon

1   Tbs blackstrap molasses

1. Cream together bananas, shortening, and sugar. Add beaten eggs and cream again. Add flour, salt, baking powder, baking soda, and cinnamon. Mix well. Fold in nuts last.

2. Makes two small loaves or one large. Put in greased loaf pans and bake at 350°F for about 45 minutes or until toothpick in center comes out clean.

3. Cool before slicing.

Brioche Bread

Traditional French Brioche

Yield: 3 Lbs, 2 medium loaf pans 8"x4"

5 cups all purpose flour

1 package dry yeast

1/4 cup nonfat dry milk

1 Tbs sugar

1-1/2 tsp salt

1 cup hot water (120-130°F)

1 cup (2 sticks) butter, room temperature

5 eggs, room temperature

1. Into a large mixing or mixer bowl pour 2 cups flour, the dry ingredients, and hot water. seat in the mixer for 2 minutes at medium speed, or for an equal length of time with a large wooden spoon. Add the butter and continue beating for one minute.

2. Add the. eggs, one at a time, and the remaining flour 1/2 cup at a time, beating thoroughly with each addition. The dough will be soft and sticky, and it must be beaten until it is shiny, elastic, and pulls away from your hands.

3. If kneading by hand, grab the dough in one hand holding the bowl with the other, and pull a large handful out of the bowl, about 12-14 inches aloft, and throw it back with considerable force. Continue pulling and slapping back the dough for about 18-20 minutes. It is sticky and messy but don't despair, it will slowly begin to stretch and pull away as you work the dough. A heavy duly mixer at medium speed can do this in about 10 minutes. The flat beater is better than a dough hook for this kneading.

4. Rising: cover the bowl with plastic wrap and put in a warm place (80°-85°F) until dough has doubled in volume, 2 to 3 hours. If using fast acting dry yeast store in a warmer place to rise in less time, about 1-1/2 hours.

5. Note: if cheese, nuts, or fruit are to be added to the dough do so before chilling at this point.

6. Stir or push down the dough, place in a covered bowl in the refrigerator. This rich dough must be thoroughly chilled before it can be shaped, 4 hours or overnight.
7. After shaping the chilled dough, put on a well greased sheet pan or greased loaf pans. Preheat oven to 375°F for 20 minutes before baking. Brush the tops with egg milk glaze if desired (1 egg beaten with 1 Tbs of milk).
8. Place the pans on the middle shelf of the oven and bake until the loaves are light brown, about 35 minutes, turning the pans around midway through baking. Handle the loaves with care, they are fragile. Place the pans on a metal rack and turn on the side to loosen the loaves, gently turn out the loaves, allow to cool before handling or slicing, about 15-20 minutes.
9. Note: baking at 4,000 feet or more reduce oven temperature to 350°F.

"Wa la delicious rich egg bread!"

Processor Brioche Bread

Yield: one pound loaf

1-3/4 cups all purpose flour (or mix 1/2 flour substitute like spelt flour and 1/2 all purpose flour)

1 package dry yeast

3 Tbs sugar

1/4 tsp salt

2 large eggs room temperature

6 Tbs butter, melted (about 3 ounces)

If by hand is not for you this wonderful bread can be prepared in a food processor as follows. While the dough takes about 24 hours to fully develop, there is only about 15 minutes of actual working time.

By processor: attach the steel blade of the processor.

1. Measure the flour into the work bowl and add the yeast, sugar, and salt. Turn the machine on and off a few times to aerate. Drop in the eggs and process until mixed, about 7 seconds.
2. Start the processor and pour the melted butter through the feed lube in a steady stream. Stop processing after 20 seconds. The dough will be very sticky, like batter.
3. Rising: with a spatula, scrape the dough into a buttered mixing bowl. Cover tightly with plastic wrap and put aside at room temperature until the dough has almost tripled, about 3 hours. Note: if made with fast-rising yeast and at the recommended higher temperature, reduce the rising time by half.
4. Punch down the dough with floured hands. Refrigerate overnight covered tightly with plastic wrap to chill arid make firm before using.
5. After shaping dough into desired loaf size with floured hands, place in well oiled pan and brush top with butter. Bake at 350-375°F in a preheated oven for about 35 minutes until golden brown. Make sure to turn pan around halfway through baking time for even cooking. Remove from pan gently on wire rack by turning pan sideways and loosening the loaf. Allow to cool 10 to 15 minutes before further handling.

French Croissant

A combination of flours works well with this recipe. Note: plan to allow a total of 18 to 22 hours for this.

Yield: 24-30 pieces

1-1/2 cups (3 sticks) butter softened at room temperature, 60-65°F. If it is too cold the butter will break into rough pieces and tear the dough, if too warm it will be absorbed by the dough instead in layers.

3 Tbs flour

Dough:

3 cups all purpose flour, approximately 1 cup cake flour

2 tsp salt

2 Tbs sugar

2 packages dry yeast

1-2/3 cups hot milk (120-130°F)

1/3 cup cream warmed

1 egg plus 1 yolk beaten

Baking sheet: use one with sides to avoid butter running off pan.

Preparation; 2 to 3 hours

1. Sprinkle the 3 tablespoons flour over the butter and blend together on the work surface. On a length of foil fashion a 6 inch square of soft butter; fold over the sides of the foil to enclose. Place in refrigerator to chill for 2 to 3 hours.

By hand or mixer: 5 minutes
While butter is chilling, prepare the dough. Both can be done several hours or even a day or two in advance of actual layering together.

2. Combine the two flours. In a large mixing bowl blend 2 cups of the 2 flours with the dry ingredients. Add the hot milk and cream and stir with a wooden spoon or the mixer flat beater to thoroughly blend the batter like dough for about 2 minutes.

3. Kneading: stir in additional flour, 1/4 cup at a time, to make a soft dough. Knead by

hand 5 minutes or by dough hook 5 minutes to form a solid mass. There is no lengthy kneading. which would toughen the otherwise tender dough.

By processor 4 minutes:

1. Prepare the butter as above.
2. Attach the steel blade of your processor. Place 2 cups of mixed flours in the work bowl arid add the dry ingredients. Pulse to mix. Pour the hot milk and cream through the feed tube. Pulse once or twice to be certain that all the dry ingredients are moistened.
3. Add the balance of the flour, 1/2 cup at a time, pulsing the machine briefly after each addition. When the mixture forms a mass and begins to clean the sides of the bowl, stop the machine. Don't over-knead!

Refrigeration: 1 hour or more to cool down the dough and allowing it to rise. Cover the bowl with plastic wrap.

Shaping:

1. Determine that both the dough and butter are at the same temperature, 65°F is ideal. The block of butter should bend but not break when bent slightly, this may mean taking the butter out of the fridge an hour or so early to reach a workable temperature. Likewise for the dough.
2. Place the dough on a floured work surface, and with your hands press it into a 10 inch square. Unwrap the block of butter and lay the block diagonally on the dough. Bring each point of dough into the center, overlapping the edges at least 1 inch. Press dough into a neat package.
3. With a heavy rolling pin, roll the dough into a rectangle approximately 8x 18 inches. If the dough oozes butter chill for a few minutes.
4. First and second turns: fold the length of dough into 3 folds, turn so that open ends are at 12 and 6 o'clock, roll again into a rectangle. This time fold both ends into the middle and then close, as one would a book. The dough will now be in 4 layers.

5. Wrap the dough in a cloth soaked with cold water that has been wrung dry. Refrigerate this wrapped dough for 1-2 hours.
6. Third turn; remove the dough from fridge and place on the floured work surface. Unwrap, roll out, and fold in three as in a letter to be mailed. This is the final turn before it is rolled out and cut into croissants.
7. Refrigerate the dough again in a dampened cloth and wrap loosely around the dough. Place the package in a plastic bag so moisture will not be pulled out of the cloth. Chill 6-8 hours or overnight.

Shaping: about 40 minutes

1. Have ready a knife or pastry cutter and a wooden yard stick if you want the pieces to be cut evenly, otherwise cut them free hand. A French croissant cutter will cut into triangles.
2. Sprinkle the work surface with flour. Roll the dough until it is approximately10x38 inch rectangle, about 1/8 inch thick evenly. The thickness is crucial to the texture of croissants. Trim irregularities to make the rectangle uniform in width. Cut the rectangle lengthwise to make two 5 inch strips. Mark each strip into a triangle, 5 inches wide on bottom using a yard stick as a guide. Cut through the dough with a pastry, pizza cutter, or knife.
3. Separate the triangles, place them on a baking sheet and chill for 15 to 20 minutes. Any time the butter softens and sticks, place the triangles in the refrigerator until they are chilled again.
4. Place the first triangle on the work surface, point away. Pull the point gently out about 3/4 inch. Roll the triangle from the bottom to the point, slightly stretching the dough sideways with your fingers as you roll. Place the croissant on the baking sheet. Touch the tip of the point to the pan but do not place the pan underneath the body of the croissant. send into a crescent or half moon shape. Repeat until the sheet is filled. Cover lightly with wax paper. If there are more croissants to bake than there are pans or oven space, cover the triangles before shaping and reserve in the refrigerator.
5. Rising: the covered croissants will double in volume at room temperature in 1 to2 hours. When the croissants are 2/3rds

raised, remove the wax paper and brush with the egg wash. Leave uncovered for the remaining rising time.

6. Preheat the oven to 450°F 15 minutes before baking. Place the sheet on the bottom shelf, after 10 minutes move to the middle or top shelf for an additional 12-15 minutes. Croissants at the edge of the pan will brown quicker than those inside, so remove them early. If using a convection oven reduce heat 50 and bake as above. Place the croissants on a rack to cool.

Viva la croissant!

Lavash (soft)

Flat Bread from the Middle East to India

4 cups bread or all purpose flour or spelt ground fine

1 package dry yeast—quick rise

2 tsp salt

I Tbs olive oil

1-1/2 cups hot water 120°-130°F

Special equipment; 1 wok, scoured clean on the outside, and an inverted bowl with gently sloping sides.

1. By hand or mixer: in a mixing or mixer bowl place 2 cups flour, yeast and salt. Mix the Tbs of oil with the hot water and pour into the flour mixture. Stir with a wooden spoon or the mixer flat beater to blend well. Add additional flour 1/2 cup at a time to form a shaggy mass of dough.

2. Kneading: turn from the bowl onto the work counter and knead with a firm push-turn-fold motion until the dough is soft and elastic, about 8 minutes. If using a dough hook, knead 5 minutes.

By processor:

1. Attach the steel blade, pour hot water and oil into the work bowl and add the yeast arid salt. Pulse on and off to mix. Remove the cover and odd 2 cups of flour. Process 10 seconds, add the balance of the flour 1/4 cup at a time processing each time to blend.
2. When the dough forms into a ball and rides on the blad, knead for 50 seconds.
3. Rising: place the dough in a greased bowl, cover tightly with plastic wrap and put in a warm place (80°-100°) until doubled in bulk, about 40 minutes. It may take half the time with quick rising yeast.
4. Shaping: turn the dough onto a floured work surface and divide into 6 or 8 pieces. First under your palm and then with a rolling pin,

shape each ball of dough into a 10 inch circle. Place the flattened dough on the back of your hands and carefully stretch the diameter to 15 inches or so (use back of hand so your fingers don't tear the dough). After shaping the dough, dust each with flour and drape them together over the cloth-covered bowl (inverted) to rest for 10 minutes.

5. Preheat the upside down wok over a medium high flame until a drop of water sizzles and bounces off the wok. Lightly brush oil over the surface.

6. Place the dough circles, one at a time, on the hot wok. Bake until light brown underneath, about 3 minutes. Be careful not to over crisp. Adjust heat if necessary. The bread should be soft and floppy.

7. Lift the bread off the wok and gently lay on a large platter covered with wax paper. Continue baking the rounds of dough turning each one over to bake on second side about 2 minutes. Stack each round flat bread upon each other on the wax paper.

This is a marvelous bread which can be used to wrap or roll around any ingredient desired; meats, veggies, cheeses, or spreads.

Chocolate Chip Banana Cookies

Yield: 6 dozen

2-1/2 cups all purpose or spelt flour

1/2 tsp salt

1/2 tsp nutmeg

1/2 tsp cinnamon

1/2 cup butter

1 egg

1 cup mashed ripe banana

2-1/2 tsp baking soda

1 tsp vinegar

6 oz. chocolate chips

1/2 cup chopped nuts

1 tsp vanilla extract

1. Sift flour, salt, nutmeg, and cinnamon into a bowl. Set aside. Cream butter and banana, gradually add sugar. Beat until light and fluffy. Add flour to mixture 1/2 cup at a time, mix well. Stir in chocolate chips and nuts, mix well.

2. Drop by teaspoonful onto lightly greased cookie sheet. Bake in 350°F oven on the middle rack until lightly browned. Cool on wire rack or cold plates.

Spelt Oatmeal Raisin Cookies

Yield: approximately 2 dozen cookies

1 cup butter softened

1 cup brown sugar

1/2 cup honey or maple syrup

2 tsp vanilla

3 Tbs milk or water

2 eggs

1 tsp baking soda

1/2 tsp salt

1-3/4 cups spelt flour

2-1/2 cups oats (quick or old fashioned)

1 cup chopped nuts or coconut flakes

3/4 cup pre-soaked raisins

1. Beat eggs and butter until creamy. Add sugar, milk, and vanilla, mix well. Add honey, baking soda, salt. Mix in oats, raisins, and nuts.
2. Drop by tablespoon onto ungreased cookie sheet.
3. Bake 10-12 minutes in a 350°F oven or until golden brown. Remove onto plate. Let cool 5 minutes.

Apple Raisin Cookies

Yield:

1 cup raisins

1/2 cup shortening or soft butter

1-1/2 cups brown sugar I egg

2 cups spelt flour

1/2 tsp salt

I tsp baking soda

1 tsp cinnamon

1 cup nuts (optional)

1 cup chopped apples

1/4 tsp ground cloves

Cook raisins in water 3 minutes, drain well. Cream sugar, shortening, and egg. Sift dry ingredients together and add raisins. Add to creamed mixture, add nuts and apples. Mix well. Drop by teaspoonful onto cookie sheet and bake 12-15 minutes at 375°F or until golden brown.

Jumbo Gingersnaps

Yield: 10 large

1/2 cup sugar

2-1/4 cups flour

3/4 cup salad or olive oil

1/4 cup dark molasses

2 tsp baking soda

1 tsp ground ginger

1/2 tsp ground cinnamon

1/2 tsp ground cardamom

1/4 tsp salt

1 large egg or 2 small eggs

1. Place all ingredients in a large mixer bowl arid mix at low speed until well blended.
2. Place at least 1/3 cup sugar in a dish. Shape 1/4 cup dough with a small ice cream dipper or tablespoon into a ball; roll in sugar to coat. Place on cookie sheet 3 inches apart.
3. Bake 14 to 15 minutes at 350°F. Makes 10 or so 4 inch cookies. Remove from pan and cool on cutting board or plates.
4. Store in airtight container.

Chocolate Soufflé

3 Tbs butter

/4 cup sifted flour

1/4 tsp salt

1 cup milk

2 ounces unsweetened or semi-sweet chocolate

4 eggs separated

1/2 cup sugar

1/4 tsp fresh cream of tartar

1. Have ready 1-1/2 quart soufflé dish. In a heavy sauce pan melt butter. Blend in flour and salt. Add milk, cook stirring constantly until thickened. Add chocolate, stir until melted. Remove from heat.
2. Beat egg yolks until thick and lemon colored. Beat sugar into yolks a little at a time. Blend chocolate into egg yolks.
3. Fold cream of tartar into stiffly beaten egg whites gently. Gently fold eaten egg whites into chocolate mixture.
4. Pour or spoon into soufflé dish, filling dish to top or at least 1/2 inch of top. Bake at 350°F for 1 hour, or until knife inserted in center comes out clean.
5. Serve topped with chocolate sauce.

Chocolate Sauce

2 ounces semi sweet chocolate

2-1/2 Tbs butter

I pinch of salt

1/2 cup brown sugar

1/4 cup boiling water or hot milk or 1/3 cup orange juice

In a small sauce pan, over low heat, melt chocolate and butter. Add sugar, water or other liquid, and salt. Bring to a boil. Cook until sauce will coat a spoon. Remove from heat. Sauce will get hard when chilled.

Spelt Pancakes

1/4 tsp ground cinnamon

1 cup spelt flour

1/2 tsp baking powder (aluminum free)

1 Tbs brown sugar or maple syrup

1 egg beaten

3/4 cup milk or water

2 tsp cold pressed safflower or olive oil or butter

1/2 tsp baking soda

Beat ingredients together, let batter stand for a while before frying. Grease the pan lightly but only once. Fry one side until bubbles appear, then turn over. Great with butter and syrup, or honey and cinnamon, also with spinach and cheese.

Spelt Tacos or Tortilla Shells

2 cups spelt flour, or 1-1/2 cups spelt flour and 1/2 cup cornmeal

1 tsp salt

1/4 cup butter

1/2 cup lukewarm water

1. Combine flour and salt. Add butter cuffing finely into small pieces, when particles are fine add water. Knead thoroughly until smooth and flecked with air bubbles.
2. Divide dough into 10 to 12 small or 6 large balls and roll as thin as possible on lightly floured board.
3. Fry on hot un-greased heavy skillet for 30 to 60 seconds until light brown. Turn over and bake on other side.
4. Serve hot or cold and freeze for later use. May be warmed up in tightly covered dish.

Note: fine chopped herbs or veggies or spices may be added to the dough for great flavors before rolling into tortillas.
Have some fun!

Spelt Garden Lavender Pound Cake

Yield: 1 loaf or 2 small loaves

1-2 Tbs dried lavender

4 eggs (room temperature)

1 cup unsalted butter (room temp.)

3/4 cup sour cream (room temp.)

2-1/2 cups spelt flour (fine) or half spelt and half wheat

1 tsp baking powder

1/2 tsp baking soda

1/4 tsp salt

2-1/2 cups sugar

1 Tbs vanilla extract

Topping:

1 cup powdered sugar (sifted)

I Tbs warm butter

3-4 tsp fresh lemon juice

1. In a spice grinder or food processor combine 1/2 cup of sugar with dried lavender—pulse 30 seconds.
2. Preheat oven 325°F.
3. In a large bowl beat the lavender—sugar, 1 cup butter, vanilla, second 1/2 cup sugar with electric mixer on high speed until very smooth, light and fluffy, about 4 minutes.
4. In a medium bowl stir together flour, baking powder, baking soda, and salt. Set aside.
5. Alternately add flour mixture and sour cream to butter mixture beating on low speed after each addition until just combined (it will be thick). Stir in lemon peel.
6. Spread mixture into prepared pan(s), well greased (two 8x4x2 inch pans or one 5x9x4 inch pan). Bake about 45 minutes or until a wooden toothpick inserted comes out clean. Cool on wire rack 10 minutes then remove from pans.
7. In a small bowl mix 1 cup sifted powdered sugar with 1 lbs butter melted with 4 teaspoons lemon juice for cake topping. Drizzle over cooled cake(s) letting it run down the sides.

Chocolate Spelt Brownies

Yield: 24 large triangles

1 pound butter

2-1/2 cups chocolate chips (semi sweet)

10 eggs

3-3/4 cups brown sugar

1-1/2 Tbs vanilla extract

1/2 tsp salt

3-1/2 cups spelt flour (ground fine)

2 cups chopped nuts (optional)

1. Preheat oven to 325°F. In a glass bowl place buffer and chocolate, cover and microwave until melted, stir smooth.
2. In a large glass bowl (8 quart) whip eggs, beat well until foamy. Add sugar, vanilla, salt arid mix thoroughly.
3. Mix in melted butter and chocolate into egg mixture. Beat well. Stir in flour until just blended with a whip. Then fold in nuts if desired.
4. Scrape into a well oiled half size baking sheet pan with 3/4 inch sides or better (12x17 inches). Smooth top with rubber spatula as evenly as possible. Bake at 325° for 40 minutes. Rotate pan and bake for 20 minutes more, or until toothpick inserted comes out clean in center of pan.
5. Cool thoroughly before portioning brownies. Trim 1/2 to 3/4 inch all the way around and discard or remove. Cut into 4x4 inch squares then cut diagonally in half. Use a metal spatula to remove gently.

Note: these brownies freeze well for weeks or months. Taste great with ice cream or whip cream.

Scones

Yield: approximately 12-16

1. Use a large bowl. Cut 1 pound of butter into small pieces 1/2 inch in size. Add to 4 cups of all purpose flour with 2 cups of spelt flour and 2 cups cake flour. Mix well.
2. Mix in:
    1/2 cup or more sugar
    4 tsp baking soda
    4 tsp baking powder
    1/2 tsp salt
    Zest from 2 lemons
    2 tsp of whatever spice you like
    2 cups of whatever fruit juice you like
3. Stir in 3 cups of buttermilk
4. Form dough into 5 ounce blobs. Arrange on well greased baking sheet pans. Bake at 325°F approximately 20 minutes or until golden on the outside and set in the middle.

Note: flavor options for suggestion:
    Orange ginger
    Cinnamon walnut
    Apple cinnamon
    Cranberry orange
    Raspberry
    Toasted almond
    Chocolate chips
    Apricot pecan

Spelt Raisin Bagels

Yield: 1 dozen

1/2 tsp quick active dry yeast

2 tsp salt

2-2/3 Tbs malt

2 tsp cinnamon

1/2 tsp nutmeg

1 tsp brown sugar

1-1/2 cups water (75°-80°F)

4 cups high gluten flour

1 cup whole grain spell flour

1. Mix all ingredients except flour and raisins until dissolved then add flour and knead for 8 minutes. Add raisins and knead for an additional 2 minutes by hand or mixer.

2. Let dough rest 10 minutes. Form into bagel shapes by portioning into 12 equal pieces. Roll out each piece using palms of hands on a lightly floured surface, rolling forward and toward you into cigar-like shapes. Bring ends together forming a circle and gently press together.

3. Let bagels rise in a warm place 80°-85° for one hour.

4. Boil bagels for 30 seconds or until they float.

5. Place on greased baking sheet pans and bake at 400°F for 10 to 15 minutes or until golden brown.

Organic Apricot Brownies

Yield: 1/2 sheet pan 12x17 inch or 3 5x9 inch loaf pans, 24 each

5 eggs

8 oz softened butter

1-1/2 Tbs olive oil

2 cups dried fresh apricots

3-3/4 cups brown sugar

3-1/2 cups spelt flour

1-1/4 tsp baking powder

1/2 tsp baking soda

1-1/2 Tbs vanilla extract

1 pinch salt

1-1/2 Tbs blackstrap molasses

1 ripe banana

1-1/2 cups pecans or walnuts (optional)

1. Cream banana, add to whipped eggs in an 11 quart bowl. Add molasses, butter, and oil.

2. Measure out flour in a separate bowl. Add baking powder, baking soda, and salt to flour, mix well.

3. Add dry mixture ingredients 1 cup at a time to the large bowl of wet ones, mix well. Fold in apricots.

4. Grease sheet pan or loaf pans with olive or safflower oil. Pour cake brownie batter in leaving 3/4 inch for rising room. Bake in preheated 350°F for about 45 minutes or until toothpick inserted comes out clean.

5. Let cool for 15 minutes before slicing. After 1-1/2 hours refrigerate or freeze brownies.

Organic Oatmeal Spelt Bread

1 large orange

7/8 cup brown sugar

1-1/2 cups spelt flour

1 Tbs baking powder

1/2 tsp salt

1/4 tsp baking soda

1 cup rolled oats

2 eggs beaten

2 Tbs melted butter

2/3 cup warm water (105°-115°F)

Use 1 large pan (9x5 inch) or two small pans (7x3 inch) greased well with butter or olive oil

1. Peel the orange and grate the rind first cutting off the white membrane or pith of the orange with a sharp knife and set aside. Cut the fruit flesh into small pieces and add the orange zest. Sprinkle with 2 tablespoons of brown sugar and set aside.

2. In a large bowl measure the flour, 3/4 cup of sugar, baking powder, salt, and baking soda. Stir in the rolled oats.

3. In a separate bowl mix the wet ingredients; the reserved orange mixture, melted butter, eggs, and water. Blend the liquid into the dry ingredients. Pour the batter into the prepared baking pan.

4. Preheat oven to 350°F while the loaf rests for 10 minutes or so. Bake the loaves or loaf until a toothpick inserted comes out clean. Large loaf takes about 1 hour, small loaves take about 45 minutes depending on the oven, always check early. Wax paper may be used in pans to facilitate easy removal of loaves. Allow to cool before slicing.

Great with butter or cinnamon.

Berry Muffins

2 cups flour

1 tsp baking soda

1/2 tsp cinnamon 1/2 tsp ground cloves

1/2 tsp ground ginger

1/2 cup butter softened

1-1/2 lbs molasses 1 egg

1 cup milk

1-1/2 cup fresh berries

1 cup nuts (optional)

1. Stir together dry ingredients and set aside.
2. Cream butter, egg, and sugar until fluffy. Add flour and milk alternately to creamed mixtures beat smooth. Fold in berries and nuts.
3. Fill well greased muffin tins 2/3 full and bake at 350°F for 35 to 40 minutes.

Banana Bread 2

1/2 cup soft butler

1 cup or less brown sugar or 3/4 cup honey or maple syrup

2 eggs beaten

2 cups spelt flour, ground fine & coarse mixed

1 tsp baking soda

1/4 tsp salt

3 ripe bananas mashed

1/2 cup chopped nuts (almonds, walnuts, or pecans)

1 tsp vanilla extract

1. Preheat oven to 350°F
2. Cream butter and sugar, add eggs and beat well. Add dry ingredients and finally bananas then nuts. Mix well.
3. Bake in three 3x5 inch loaf pans or one 5x9 inch pan well greased. Bake for 1 hour or until toothpick comes out clean. Smaller loaf pans will only take 40-45 minutes.

Spelt Applesauce Cake Bread
or Apple Spice Ginger Bread

Yield: 1 loaf

1 cup canned or homemade applesauce

1 apple diced 1/4 inch

1 cup brown sugar

1 Tbs blackstrap molasses

1/2 cup butter melted

2 cups spelt flour

1/2 tsp salt

1 tsp cinnamon

1/4 tsp nutmeg

1/2 tsp allspice

1/2 tsp ground ginger

1/2 tsp ground cloves

1/4 tsp baking soda

1/2 tsp baking powder

1 egg beaten well

1/4 cup milk or water

1 tsp vanilla

1. Cream butter and egg into applesauce with sugar and molasses. Add salt, cinnamon, nutmeg, ginger, cloves, allspice, baking powder and baking soda last. Mix well with water or milk (1/4 cup or so) and vanilla.
2. Sauté diced apples in an additional tablespoon of butter then fold into bowl. Add flour 1/2 cup at a time just until blended. Do not over mix.
3. Pour batter into 5x9 inch greased loaf pan and bake at 350°F for 30 to 45 minutes or until toothpick comes out clean.
4. Serve warm or cold.

Cinnamon Rolls

Yield: 9 rolls

1. Combine:
    2 Tbs active dry yeast
    1/2 cup warm water
    2 tsp sugar
2. Mix together:
    7 Tbs brown sugar
    4 eggs
    5-1/2 ounces melted butter
    1 cup sour cream
    1-1/2 tsp vanilla
    1 tsp salt
3. Mix these two parts together. Incorporate 7 to 8 cups of flour a little at a time until well blended. Put in a warm covered spot, let rise (proof) until double in size, about 45 minutes to 1 hour.
4. Roll into rectangle, then spread a layer of soft butter all over the rectangle. Sprinkle generously with sugar and cinnamon, at least another 1/2 cup of brown sugar. Roll and pinch seam. Cut into 2 inch slices.
5. Lay onto oiled baking sheet and let rise until puffy. Bake at 325°F 9-12 minutes. Watch carefully, they cook quickly.
6. Top with a mixture of honey, brown sugar, cinnamon, and melted butter. Drizzle over the tops and serve.

Tips

Special Notes: What To Do

♦ Crust too hard: if the crust is too hard and crisp, next time bake with less steam in the oven. A hard crust will soften overnight in a plastic bag.

♦ Crust too soft: if the crust is too soft for example, French type bread, more water added to the broiler pan will generate more steam, or give it an additional spray of water with an atomizer. A swipe with a wet pastry brush will also help to develop a hard crust.

♦ Poorly baked: the dough was beautifully risen when it went into the oven but it came out a disappointment. Test the oven thermometer with a baking thermometer, never trust the oven thermometer alone.

♦ Shelling or splitting: when the bread under the top crust separates to form a tunnel or splits the length of the loaf, is caused by one or two things. The top of the dough may have been partially dried out during the rising and later during the baking the heat could not penetrate the thick surface of the dough shell, or the oven heat expanded the dough unevenly. Next time cover the dough during rising with wax paper parchment or foil to prevent loss of moisture, check temperature of oven and always preheat the oven.

♦ Uneven crust color: it's always good to change the position of the loaves in the oven once or twice during baking to ensure even browning.

♦ A layered effect: if there is a layer of dough in the loaf just below the crust that is different in texture and color when baked, it may be that you added too much flour too late in the kneading process and it didn't get absorbed into the dough. I recommend on the next batch try to knead well after all the flour is added.

♦ Salt: when the loaf is baked and the slice tastes flat, you probably have forgotten the salt. Also if made without salt the dough will be unresponsive, stringy, and pull away in strands. Salt helps the yeast and kneading process. Salt water may be brushed on the bread after it is baked.

In my next book, "Sauces For Any Occasion", we will delight the taste buds further. The sauce "makes" the dish. Soups, dinner, and dessert sauces for defining worldly recipes from old world traditional sauces to contemporary, with some fresh new ideas and creative dishes.

Enjoy making up your own recipes to suit your desires of imagination and flavors preferred. Wholegrain spelt flour in fine baked breads and cakes.

BVG